EXTREME WEATHER

TORNADOES

by Liza Burby

The Rosen Publishing Group's
PowerKids Press™
New York

Published in 1999 by The Rosen Publishing Group, Inc.
29 East 21st Street, New York, NY 10010

First Edition

Book Design: Resa Listort

Photo Credits: Cover © ; p. 4 © Ambrose, Paul & Lindamarie/FPG International; pp. 7, 10, 16, 19 © Warren Faidley/International Stock; p. 8 © 1997 Digital Vision Ltd.; p. 12 © Tony Arruza/Tony Arruza Photography, Inc.; p. 15 © Bob Firth/International Stock; p. 20 © Seth Dinnerman; p. 20 © 1997 Digital Vision Ltd.

Burby, Liza N..
      Tornadoes / by Liza N. Burby.
            p.   cm. — (Extreme weather)
      Includes index.
      Summary: An introduction to the storms sometimes known as twisters, including how and where they occur, the damage they can do, and some of the worst tornadoes in recorded history.
      ISBN 0-8239-5289-4
      1. Tornadoes—Juvenile literature. [1. Tornadoes.]
      I. Title. II. Series.
QC955.2.B87 1998
551.55'3—dc21   97-52012
                                                                                       CIP
                                                                                       AC

Manufactured in the United States of America

Contents

What Is a Tornado?

Seeing a tornado can be very exciting. But it can also be very scary too. **Meteorologists** (MEE-tee-oh-RAHL-uh-jists) say a tornado is the most **violent** (VY-oh-lent) of all storms. Sometimes it is also called a twister or **cyclone** (SY-klohn).

A tornado looks like a giant swirling, spinning cloud. Part of the cloud is shaped like a **funnel** (FUN-ul) and looks almost like a finger pointing to the ground. This part is called the **vortex** (VOR-teks). It can hang straight down and look like it's not moving at all. It can wiggle gently in the air. It can even wave like a whip. A tornado is very **dangerous** (DAYN-jer-us).

Wide open spaces, such as the plains of the United States, are perfect places for tornadoes to start.

Where and When Do They Happen?

Many parts of the world have tornadoes. In the United States, there are about 1,000 tornadoes each year. Because most of these tornadoes happen in one area, that part of the United States is called the tornado playground. The area, which includes the states of Colorado, Kansas, Montana, Nebraska, New Mexico, North Dakota, Oklahoma, South Dakota, Texas, and Wyoming is also known as Tornado Alley. During tornado season, which usually happens during April, May, and June, twenty to forty tornadoes can occur each week.

People who live in the tornado playground usually have strong cellars to keep them safe during a tornado. ▶

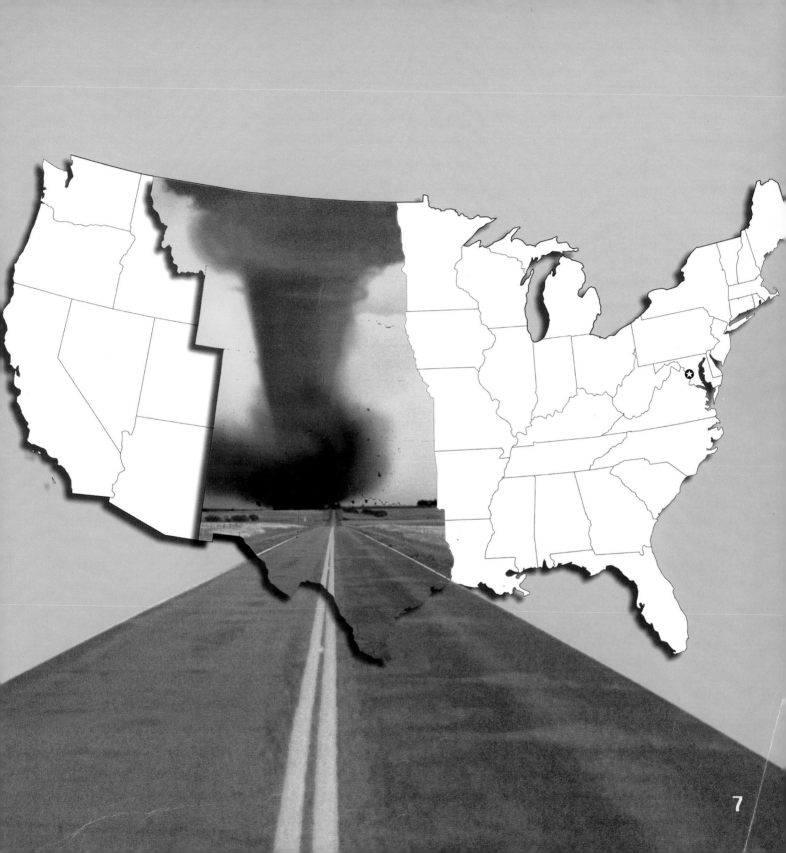

How Do They Start?

Meteorologists don't know all the reasons why we have tornadoes. But they do know that tornadoes usually start if there is a bad thunderstorm with lightning, **hail** (HAYL), and fast winds. Tornadoes often happen during the warmest part of the day, or between 4:00 pm and 6:00 pm. When it is hot and **humid** (HYOO-mid), cold air can get trapped above the warm air in a storm. The cold air will try to move away from the warm air. This creates a big, black cloud. Inside the cloud, the air starts to spin.

◀ Bright lightning can be seen during summer thunderstorms. Sometimes a tornado will follow.

How Do Tornadoes Act?

Because tornado winds spin so fast, they make a **vacuum** (VAK-yoom). This vacuum acts like your vacuum at home, but instead of just dirt, it sucks up and moves things like trees and cars! Tornadoes make buzzing, hissing, whistling, or roaring sounds. Even though they can make these scary sounds, they're usually not very big. In fact, tornadoes can be very skinny. They only stay in one place for a minute before spinning off to a new spot. They may skip or hop over spots, moving about 20 to 50 miles per hour. In less than 30 minutes tornadoes usually lose their strength and disappear.

A tornado changes direction quickly, so you may not know where it will go next.

A Water Tornado

Sometimes a tornado can happen at sea. This is called a **waterspout** (WAH-ter-spowt). It starts over lakes and oceans. The waterspout sucks a long **column** (KOL-um) of water from the ocean into the sky.

Waterspouts occur off the East Coast of the United States, in the Gulf of Mexico, in China, and in Japan. The winds of a waterspout are not as strong as the winds of a tornado on land. But these tornadoes are strong enough to pull fish and frogs from the water and carry them to other places. On July 13, 1949, in a town in New Zealand, thousands of fish "rained" on a farm because of a waterspout!

From the shore, a waterspout, such as this one in the Florida Keys, can look like a skinny ladder leading into the sky.

Tornadoes Do Strange Things

One reason people are interested in tornadoes is because they do weird things. A tornado once lifted a train full of people off its tracks and carried it through the air. During another twister, a man was wrapped up in a wire fence. One family watched as their house was smashed and carried away by a tornado. Then the floor of the house gently floated out of the sky and landed exactly where it had been!

Tornadoes are a very strange part of nature. They have been known to take the feathers off a chicken and carry big cows from one farm to another. Some cows have even disappeared during a tornado!

Tornadoes can do incredible and scary things, such as turn houses upside down!

The Worst Tornadoes

Tornadoes can wreck houses, cars, and other things. Sometimes they even hurt and kill people. In 1990, a wild tornado blew into Illinois before meteorologists knew about it. The meteorologists couldn't warn people in time. Many people were hurt, and some even died. On April 3rd and 4th in 1974, 148 tornadoes hit fourteen states. This is the largest number of tornadoes ever to come from one thunderstorm. One of the worst tornadoes in history was the Great Tri-State tornado of 1925. It moved across the states of Missouri, Illinois, and Indiana and lasted three and a half hours. That's a long time for a tornado! When it was over, 689 people had died and 1,500 were hurt.

A tornado can do a little or a huge amount of damage, as seen in this photo of what a tornado did in Texas.

Looking for Tornadoes

Because tornadoes can hurt people, meteorologists try to figure out when one is coming. They watch for weather **patterns** (PAT-ernz) so they can warn people. These patterns can **predict** (pre-DIKT) the weather. Meteorologists use **instruments** (IN-struh-ments) to watch for the patterns. Some instruments measure movement in the clouds. Others measure air **temperature** (TEMP-rah-chur) and wind speed. People called spotters also help. They go outside looking for a tornado so they can warn people in time. Tornado chasers like to follow and watch tornadoes. They are very careful, and take pictures of the ones they see. These pictures help meteorologists learn more about tornadoes.

This picture, taken from the NWS Doppler radar 88-D, shows a tornado's location in gold. ▶

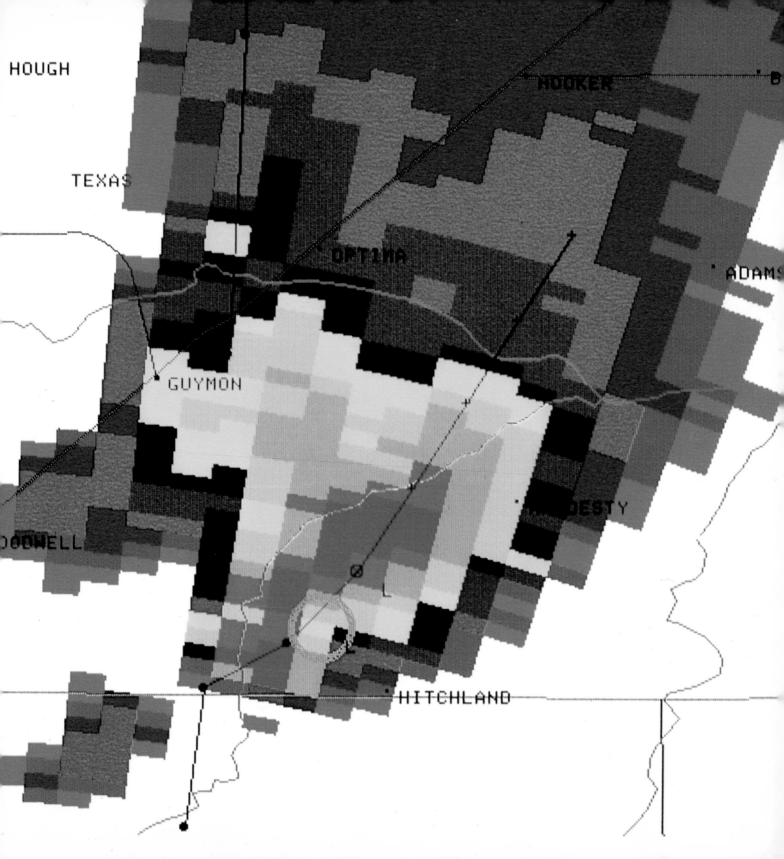

How Do You Know If It's Coming?

Tornadoes are scary, but you can usually find out if one is coming. You may see a bad thunderstorm with thunder and lightning and strong winds and hail. You might hear a roaring sound. If this happens, listen to your radio or TV for news reports about a possible tornado. If the radio or TV says there is a tornado watch, you should watch the sky. Be ready to go to a safe place if a tornado warning is announced. A tornado warning means that meteorologists have spotted a tornado and they know where it is heading.

A thunderstorm doesn't always mean that a tornado is on the way. But it's better to be safe than sorry. If possible, stay inside during a heavy storm.

Safety During a Tornado

If you are home alone during a tornado warning, go to your basement and hide under a heavy piece of furniture. If you don't have a basement, get into a closet in the middle of the house. Keep away from all windows in case the glass breaks. If you are outside and you can't reach **shelter** (SHEL-ter), lie flat in a ditch. Cover your head with your hands to protect yourself from flying glass and dirt. Learn about your state's tornado safety rules. It will help keep you safe from these violent storms.

Tornadoes are interesting and sometimes beautiful parts of nature. Meterologists are learning more and more every day about the weather and our world from these twisters. But we must also remember that they can be dangerous. Tornadoes should be respected as the powerful storms that they are.

Glossary

column (KOL-um) Something that is tall and skinny.

cyclone (SY-klohn) Another name for a tornado.

dangerous (DAYN-jer-us) Causing harm.

funnel (FUN-ul) Something that is wide at the top and thin at the bottom.

hail (HAYL) Small, round pieces of ice that sometimes fall during a thunderstorm.

humid (HYOO-mid) Damp or moist.

instrument (IN-struh-ment) A tool used in doing or learning something.

meteorologist (MEE-tee-oh-RAHL-uh-jist) A scientist who studies the weather.

pattern (PAT-ern) Something that happens again and again.

predict (pre-DIKT) To know something before it happens.

shelter (SHEL-ter) A safe place.

temperature (TEMP-rah-chur) How hot or cold something is.

vacuum (VAK-yoom) Something that sucks up whatever is near it.

violent (VY-oh-lent) Strong, rough force.

vortex (VOR-teks) The part of the tornado cloud that points to the ground.

waterspout (WAH-ter-spowt) A tornado that happens over a lake or ocean.

Index